A Brief History of
Feminism

A Brief History of
Feminism

PATU / ANTJE SCHRUPP

translated by Sophie Lewis

The MIT Press / Cambridge, Massachusetts / London, England

First MIT Press paperback edition, 2024
This translation © 2017 Massachusetts Institute of Technology

Originally published as *Kleine Geschichte des Feminismus im euro-amerikanischen Kontext,*
© UNRAST-Verlag, Münster

This book was set in Myriad Pro and Adobe Garamond Pro by The MIT Press. Printed and bound in the United States of America.

Library of Congress Cataloging-in-Publication Data

Names: Schrupp, Antje, 1964– author. | Patu, (Illustrator)
Title: A brief history of feminism / Patu and Antje Schrupp ; translated by Sophie Lewis.
Other titles: Kleine Geschichte des Feminismus. English
Description: Cambridge, MA : MIT Press, [2017]
Identifiers: LCCN 2017008083 | ISBN 9780262037112 (hardcover : alk. paper)—9780262548670 (paperback)
Subjects: LCSH: Feminism—History.
Classification: LCC HQ1121 .S3313 2017 | DDC 305.4209—dc23 LC record available at https://lccn.loc.gov
/2017008083

10   9   8   7   6   5

EVE AND ADAM, OR WHAT IS FEMINISM ANYWAY?

Practically every culture claims a fundamental difference between human genders or sexes. Usually, though not always, it's a question of just two: male and female. The principle of two sexes was elaborated in the Bible's account of creation, the story of Adam and Eve.

> And the Lord God caused a deep sleep to fall upon Adam, and he slept: and he took one of his ribs, and closed up the flesh instead thereof; And the rib, which the Lord God had taken from man, made he a woman, and brought her unto the man. And Adam said, This is now bone of my bones, and flesh of my flesh: she shall be called Woman, because she was taken out of Man.

This is often interpreted today to mean that man was created first, and then woman, "from his rib." But actually, the Hebrew word "Adam" is not the name of a man; it is simply the word for "human being." Adam had no gender in the very beginning. The creation of Eve, then, did not so much introduce woman into the world as gender difference. Out of the gender-neutral human being "Adam" came man and woman.

Equating Adam with man already shows us the root of the problem: in many cultures, actual men are equated with man as such. Some languages even have only one word for both (*homme* in French, for example). Men implicitly stand for humanity, whereas women are considered to be somehow derivative, deficient, inferior human beings.

The practical consequences vary depending on the region of the world, the prevailing ideology, and the era: women may have, for example, fewer rights, less money, minimal experience of public life, and limited access to positions of power. Or—in emancipated societies—if they are considered to be "equals," they are still measured against a male norm.

This primacy of the male is called *patriarchy* (literally: rule by the father) and it exists in many variants. Its core hierarchy structures almost every other form of power, not just the relationship between the genders: the head of the household over his children, maids, and servants; the free man over slaves; "natives" over immigrants; the "better off" over the "lower classes," and so on.

Understanding the causes of patriarchy and how exactly it has come about has been controversial. Some believe it is the result of historical developments that began about 5,000 years ago with the gradual displacement of early indigenous cultures. Some believe patriarchy is the inevitable consequence of the fact that not everyone can get pregnant and give birth, resulting in a gendered division of labor that emerged at the expense of women. Others reject the term "patriarchy" altogether because it gathers too many diverse phenomena under one label.

Indeed, there is such a variety of "patriarchal" societies that the term is insufficient for the purposes of analyzing concrete conditions. But they do all have something in common. Every patriarchal society has feminism—which is to say, they have a number of people, more often women than men, who reject the notion that the masculine is superior to the feminine in their culture and who argue for the liberation of women.

Feminism is not so much a fixed program as an attitude. Feminists see gender difference as an important analytic tool without which social processes and relations cannot be understood. Their activism is guided by the criterion of the liberation of women, and this liberation has a value for them per se: an aim that needs no further justification.

Apart from this, different feminists have very different and sometimes even opposing points of view. These viewpoints are always shaped by specific issues and the specific problems of the time—and, of course, by the subjective ideas and views of the thinker or activist concerned.

To understand feminist ideas, then, we must always look at them in their proper context and not boil them down to one simple definition. Individuals will inevitably have to form their own judgments and take their own positions. There can be no one "feminism." New propositions, discoveries, and findings are emerging all the time.

Some of these ideas and developments are laid out in this book. The focus here is European, Western feminism, because that's the tradition in which the authors are knowledgeable and, thus, the discourse to which this book belongs. Feminism has long existed everywhere else in the world, but that feminism may look quite different from the feminism presented here.

A Brief History of
Feminism

ANTIQUITY

The very earliest known texts from ancient Europe—ancient Greece and ancient Rome to be precise—are already the texts of patriarchal societies. Therefore, nearly all of the philosophical and political ideas that have come down to us are men's ideas; only very few texts from this period can be definitely identified as authored by women. The ideas women dreamt up, the concerns they prioritized at the time, the thoughts they had on human coexistence—unfortunately, we have to remain in the dark about all that.

Yes, and that's a good thing too. A man who teaches a woman how to read or write is ill-advised, for he is providing extra venom to an asp.

Menander, 342/341 BC, Greek playwright

We do have some fragmentary traces of certain women. For example, we know that a poet called Sappho lived on the isle of Lesbos in the 7th or 6th century BCE. She wrote poems about love and sensuality.

We also know a little about the philosopher Ptolemais, who wrote a book on the "Pythagorean principles of music" around the 3rd century BCE. Plato also mentions the philosopher Diotima, allegedly a teacher of Socrates, but her historical existence has not been verified.

The Hebrew Bible features several important women, such as the prophet Miriam and the political leader Esther. There are also important women in the New Testament such as the Apostles Junia, Thekla, and Mary Magdalene.

And the mathematician Hypatia taught in Alexandria in the 4th century CE. She was murdered in the year 415 by fanatical Christian monks.

Because we have no substantive texts from this period we can say women authored with 100% certainty, we can only indirectly infer what women's ideas actually were.

For instance, take a look at a moment from the life of the early Christian missionary Paul:

Right, before I forget, this is very important: Women should be SILENT in church congregations.

Whereas in reality . . .

Paul's rebuke would not have been necessary if women had, in fact, always been silent in church.

Throughout antiquity, men penned texts admonishing women to lead a chaste life, to submit to men and especially their husbands, to fulfill their domestic duties, not make any demands, and so on.

The fact that these injunctions were necessary shows that there was, at least, some controversy around the matter, and that women didn't all simply fall in line.

As I keep saying: A woman should be seen and not heard. Somehow it hasn't had much effect.

Sophocles, 5th cent. BCE, Greek poet

There seems to have been a somewhat broader discussion about the role of women in society during the 2nd and 3rd centuries. Some of the texts from the philosophical school of "Gnosticism" elaborate the idea of a quasi-ungendered spirituality and knowledge that women can attain too, if they "become like men."

And how, if you please, was that supposed to work? Perhaps like this?

Ha ha! You can't be as enlightened as us! You don't have a penis.

Dear God, I'm just a weak woman, but please help me become male!

Okay, just this once!

FEMINISM IN THE MIDDLE AGES

In the Middle Ages, Christianity gradually became the predominant worldview in Europe.

Look out, here come the Christians!

God chose me to be his representative on Earth!

No he didn't! He chose meee!

They're getting on my nerves! I think I'll hang out with you.

Although the church was a strictly hierarchical and purely male organization, many women refused to subordinate themselves to this hierarchy. They did not reject Christianity wholesale, however. Instead, they claimed a form of direct access to God, independent from the clergy—through visions, for example, and mystical insights. They often justified this by arguing that a church doctrine created by men could never be valid for them as women.

For example, the German Abbess Hildegard von Bingen (1098–1170) engaged in numerous conflicts with the reigning powers (both secular and ecclesiastical) of her time. She invoked visions, which gave her insight into a higher, cosmological order.

If God is male, then the male is God.

Right on, man!

Mary Daly (1928–2010), originally a Catholic theologian, was one of the most important thinkers in feminist theology in the 20th century. Her 1973 book *Beyond God the Father* influenced many women. Daly herself later turned her back on the church.

Many mystics claimed that it was easier for women to "have direct access to God" (today we would say: "know what action is right") because they had no involvement in the secular power structures.

Some openly challenged the church hierarchy. One such woman was Wilhelmina of Milan, who had a vision in 1280.

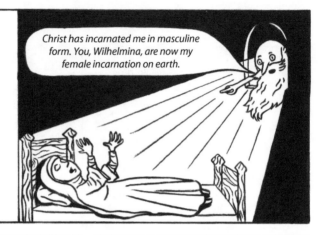

Christ has incarnated me in masculine form. You, Wilhelmina, are now my female incarnation on earth.

Two years later . . .

Mayfreda, I'm going to die soon. Finish what I have started. You must create a church with a female hierarchy.

However, Wilhelmina's followers were denounced to the Inquisition and Mayfreda was burned as a heretic in 1300.

Generally speaking, from the 13th century on, women in Europe demonstrated a stronger need for community life—life beyond marriage and monasteries. Women lived together in pairs or in smaller collectives, working together, or else formed larger organized convents with up to one hundred members. Others traveled through the country, singly or in groups.

Soon "Beguines" came into being. Some of these communities had no fixed rules, while others had very precise contracts for those who wished to join them. Most of the Beguine convents were financed by the work of their members, whether in the craft sector, in nursing care, or in trade.

One of the best-known Beguines was the Frenchwoman Marguerite Porete (ca. 1260–1310), who wrote the first major spiritual work in the vernacular language (instead of Latin). *The Mirror of Simple Souls* describes how "God" can be found only through "love," not through the church, nor through reason or virtue. Everything depends on the individual's ability to love, that is, to do the right thing in a specific, concrete situation. Laws and abstract rules do not contribute to the good in the world—as such, we might even consider Marguerite Porete an early anarchist. *The Mirror* is not a philosophical tract, but outlines a down-to-earth, experimental praxis (quite similar, in fact, to the literature of the women's movement in the 1970s).

Paris, Whitsun, 1310

Despite widespread repression, her book's influence grew. Latin, English, and Italian translations had already appeared in the 14th century.

While it had tolerated them at first, the church stepped up its persecution of the Beguines in the 14th and 15th centuries. Eventually almost all of the women's collectives were crushed or else forced to transform themselves into monasteries operating under strict ecclesiastical control. Nevertheless, some Beguine communes did survive, all the way into the 19th century.

Even within the newly "official" nunneries, distinct women-led traditions survived. The Spanish abbess Teresa of Ávila (1515–1582), for example, drew up her own rules for the monasteries she founded, because she believed that the orders for men, having been designed by men, were not suitable for women. An inquisitorial proceeding was initiated against her order, but eventually the church recognized her doctrines as orthodox, and canonized Teresa in 1622. In 1970 she became (posthumously) the first woman ever to become a Doctor of the Church.

We should not assess feminist ideas using the criteria of currently dominant ideologies. Just as the medieval church burned many progressive-thinking women at the stake while declaring others saints, neoliberal society now adopts some feminist ideas with gusto, while marginalizing others as totally utopian.

During the Reformation in the 16th century, many nunneries were forcibly disbanded. The women who had been living in them were compelled to marry in order to survive, which in turn meant that many areas suffered the near-total collapse of their independent traditions and ways of life.

A new generation of feminist theologians had to rediscover many of these traditions in the 20th century, since the official church historiographies did not mention them.

EARLY MODERN FEMINISM

In the modern period, ideas of the nation-state, rule of law, and science gradually displaced Christian beliefs. Sadly, however, this did not mean that the standing of women all of a sudden improved. Because, you see, men could now supposedly argue the case for women's inferiority "objectively" . . .

One of the most important feminists of the early modern period whose life and work we still know of today was the French philosopher and writer Christine de Pizan (1365–1430). In 1405 she published *The Book of the City of Ladies*, in which she deftly attacks, with an exquisite sense of irony, the misogynist thinking of many of her contemporaries, especially the popular notion that women have fewer aptitudes and are less capable than men.

"They who defame women are small spirits. They have encountered so many women ranking far above them in terms of wisdom and gentility, that their reaction is to be sulky and indignant. And because of this grudge, they speak ill of all women."
—Christine de Pizan

In *City of Ladies* Pizan pays tribute to numerous biblical or historical women and paints a picture of a utopian society in which all women are free and enjoy the same rights as men.

The book represents one of the less typical contributions to the so-called Woman Question, a Europe-wide debate over the essence and status of women, which lasted from the 14th right through to the 18th century. The spectrum of opinion ranged from those who outright denied that women are people and saw women as being on a level with animals, all the way to those who defended the dignity of women and championed their freedom.

In general, perspectives on the "Woman Question" became more polarized in this period. On the one hand, hatred of women increased, and this found its ultimate expression in the persecution of witches. On the other hand, subcultures developed in which women could have relatively powerful influence, for example, the "Précieuses," a movement among the nobility.

An important early thinker in this movement was the French philosopher Marie de Gournay (1565–1645).

A logical consequence is the right of women to be human, for in principle the human spirit is neither masculine nor feminine.

Biological differences in sex do not account for the spirit of a human being, rather, they serve only for procreation. After all, this female cat on my windowsill cannot be distinguished from a tomcat.

Her book *The Equality of Men and Women* appeared in 1622. It's a very early example of modern "equal rights" discourse: a truly visionary text for its time.

Indeed, in a strongly hierarchical society that was divided into "estates," the very idea of equality (not just between sexes, but among human beings in general) was seen as completely absurd. Gournay suffered a lot of scorn and derision in the wake of her intervention.

"Most of those who take up the cause of women, opposing the arrogant preference for themselves that is asserted by men, give them full value for money, for they redirect the preference to them. For my part, I fly all extremes, I am content to make them equal to men."—Marie de Gournay

FEMINISM IN THE ENLIGHTENMENT

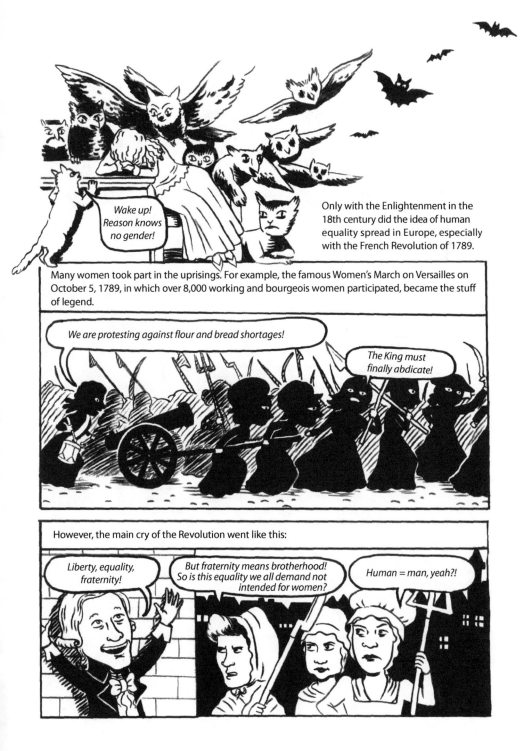

Wake up! Reason knows no gender!

Only with the Enlightenment in the 18th century did the idea of human equality spread in Europe, especially with the French Revolution of 1789.

Many women took part in the uprisings. For example, the famous Women's March on Versailles on October 5, 1789, in which over 8,000 working and bourgeois women participated, became the stuff of legend.

We are protesting against flour and bread shortages!

The King must finally abdicate!

However, the main cry of the Revolution went like this:

Liberty, equality, fraternity!

But fraternity means brotherhood! So is this equality we all demand not intended for women?

Human = man, yeah?!

"I may excite laughter, by dropping an hint, which I mean to pursue some future time, for I really think women ought to have representatives, instead of being arbitrarily governed without having any direct share allowed them in the deliberations of government."

—Mary Wollstonecraft

In 1818, Mary Shelley (daughter of Mary Wollstonecraft) wrote the international best-seller *Frankenstein*, a masterpiece on the hubris of modern science that remains relevant to this day.

From the beginning, feminists have protested against the idea that one might posit human equality as an ideal while simultaneously excluding half of humanity. Two of the best known are Mary Wollstonecraft and Olympe de Gouges.

As early as 1790 the English teacher and writer Mary Wollstonecraft (1759–1797) wrote a book on human rights. In 1792 she traveled to Paris to get a sense of the consequences of the Revolution on the ground.

Woman is expressly made to please man.

Jean-Jacques Rousseau (1712–1778), French philosopher

Just you wait 'til my new book comes out, Jean-Jacques!

In Paris she wrote *A Vindication of the Rights of Women*. In so doing she was one of the first to criticize the fact that women were raised and socialized to be dependents. She was elaborating an argument that for many feminists remains pressing to this day: that the actually existing differences between men and women don't have "natural" causes but are produced, in the first instance, by society.

16

In 1791, the French artist and human rights activist Marie Gouze (1748–1793), better known by her pen name Olympe de Gouges, wrote the *Declaration of the Rights of Woman and the Female Citizen*.

She had been forced into marriage at seventeen and developed her political consciousness at an early age. Even before the French Revolution she campaigned for the abolition of slavery, divorce rights, and other social issues.

Her best-known "bon mot"—a woman who has the right to ascend to the scaffold must also have the right to ascend a political platform—came all too true for Olympe de Gouges. On account of her political opinions on Robespierre's regime of terror, like so many others, she was executed by guillotine in 1793.

At the beginning of the 19th century it became clearer and clearer that the idea of the "equality of all men" had not only widened the chasm between men and women . . .

. . . but also that between rich and poor.

I'm sure we can get more than 15 hours a day out of this lot!

For political equality did not reflect the real conditions of life. Rather, it only provided the rich with even more of an excuse to focus exclusively on their own interests . . .

Poverty? Not my fault! Every man forges his own destiny. At the end of the day, we are all equal before the law.

—or, as Anatole France put it: *"In its majestic equality, the law forbids rich and poor alike to sleep under bridges, beg in the streets, and steal loaves of bread."*

The insufficiency of legal equality was the reason why various socialist movements came into being, whose dreams of equality pointed to a greater social and material kind of justice. Some socialists founded communes and projects in which they experimented with new forms of working and living together.

What is remarkable about this historic movement is not only the sheer number of women who were personally active in it, but the fact that almost *all* early socialist theories and projects explicitly addressed the question of the relation between the sexes. The gender question played an especially central role in Saint-Simonism, among the followers of the sociologist Henri de Saint-Simon, who died in 1825.

Buchez, I say to you: the new world will be governed by a papal couple. The female pope will represent emotion and the male pope reason. It's the only way a peaceful society can arise.

That man must liberate woman, and that women must be represented in all public offices, are things that we all agree on.

But there's one thing you're mistaken about, Enfantin: what you call gender-specific characteristics are not in fact "given" by nature, but rather, are attributable to unequal socialization.

While the men were still quarreling . . .

I've had enough of these men who think they can speak for us.

Yes, Saint-Simonism is still colored by male perspectives.

Let's publish our own newspaper and set up women's groups.

Some Saint-Simonist women signaled their revolutionary thinking via daring forms of vestimentary self-expression, for example by wearing noticeably short skirts, which displayed the fact that they were wearing trousers underneath.

Among the important Saint-Simonist women were Claire Démar (1799–1833) and Jeanne Deroin (1805–1894).

> Precisely because woman is equal to man but not identical to him, she should participate in the effort for social reforms, and in so doing she will embody the necessary elements that man lacks, such that the endeavor can be complete.

Jeanne Deroin

They developed models for gender-conscious organizational structures and founded autonomous women's groups. In general, the Saint-Simonists insisted that every public office and function be occupied in each case by one man and one woman. In 1850, Deroin went to jail for six months on charges of political conspiracy.

> State your first and last name!

> Before I answer, I must protest against the law by which you propose to judge me. It has been been made by men and I do not recognize its authority.

Their main argument for equal rights was that women can never be truly represented by men and must have their own voice, on the grounds that men and women are different and do not have the same preferences and interests. In this, they were reacting to the lack of contemporary theorizing on formal equality.

The most important theorist of early socialism was Flora Tristan (1803–1844). In 1825 she fled her violent husband.

I may have no legal option to get a divorce, but there's no way in hell I'm staying here.

He pursued her with all available legal means and later even made an attempt on her life.

Her revolutionary ideas must be stopped. I'll kill her before she destroys the foundations of our society!

Tristan fought back, rallying support and causing a great stir in France.

On a trip to Peru, where her family had property, Tristan rebelled against slavery and class exploitation.

STOP!!

He deserves it. He stole from me and lied about it.

As though enslaving humans were not the greatest theft imaginable! Can you expect virtue from someone who isn't allowed to have free will of their own?

The slave doesn't owe his or her master anything, and on the contrary, has the right to move against him in any way.

23

> *The working class must free itself. It can only become free through its own actions.*

In 1840, she traveled to London and researched the living conditions of workers under capitalism. She reflected on both of these experiences in her books.

"Workers, try hard to understand this: the law that subjugates women and deprives them of education oppresses you, you, proletarian men."—Flora Tristan

In 1843—five years before Marx and Engels published *The Communist Manifesto*—Tristan's main oeuvre *The Workers' Union* was published, in which she not only championed the idea of a union of male and female workers that would transcend guilds and professional branches, but also drew an analytic link between the oppression of women and the oppression of the proletariat. She promoted her ideas throughout France via lecture tours, up until her early death from typhoid in 1844.

> *Tristan? Never heard of her!*

> *No, you remember, she's—*

> *SHHH!*

BEGINNINGS OF AN ORGANIZED WOMEN'S MOVEMENT

Up until the middle of the 19th century, individual feminist actors and women's groups had certainly mobilized around specific issues, or unionized in certain trades. But there hadn't been anything like an organized women's movement.

THE FIRST CONVENTION EVER CALLED TO DISCUSS THE Civil and Political Rights of Women Seneca Falls, N.Y. JULY 19, 20, 1848 WOMEN'S RIGHTS CONVENTION

Accordingly it caused quite a stir when US feminists organized a two-day conference in the state of New York.

The two initiators . . .

In almost all congresses and political debates women are not allowed to participate as delegates, and sometimes may not even enter the room! In future this has to stop, Elizabeth!

Exactly, my dear! Our goal will be to get women more social and political influence.

Lucrezia Mott (1793–1880), women's rights activist and Quaker.

Elizabeth Cady Stanton (1815–1902), civil and women's rights activist.

Approximately 300 people interested parties attended the Seneca Falls Convention and supported its demands, including some men—for example, the black civil rights activist Frederick Douglass (1818–1895).

At the end of the convention, a "Declaration of Rights and Sentiments" was adopted, revoking all claims to power over women, in explicit reference to the American Declaration of Independence.

"We insist that women have immediate admission to all the rights and privileges which belong to them as citizens of these United States. In entering upon the great work before us, we anticipate no small amount of misconception, misrepresentation, and ridicule; but we shall use every instrumentality within our power to effect our object."—Elizabeth Cady Stanton

In Europe, too, feminists set up numerous women's associations in the second half of the 19th century, and several national and international assemblies took place. At the same time, among male intellectuals, an increasingly "antifeminist" mood began to spread. This backlash was antifeminist in the original sense of the word: namely, "against women."

WOMEN'S RIGHTS ARE HUMAN RIGHTS!

Just look at how ugly they make Europe, man! "Women's lib" is one of Europe's worst modern developments.

Pah! AS IF they were capable of working for the public good!

Political activists, writers, and intellectuals such as Jules Michelet, Pierre-Joseph Proudhon, Auguste Comte, and many many others, rejected women's demands for political and social codetermination.

Quite right, Pierre! After all, we know the results of plenty of scientific studies on the feminine physical constitution and psyche.

Gentlemen, I'm enchanted to be among like minds. May I present to you my work "On the Physiological Idiocy of Women"? One further proof of the fact that women should not study.

Paul Julius Moebius
(1853–1907)

27

This concentrated wave of antiwoman sentiment provoked, in turn, a wave of feminist literature. Feminists took apart the crude propositions of the antifeminists, both seriously and, on occasion, lightheartedly, through the use of sarcasm. Particularly popular in France was an essay by Juliette Adam (1836–1936) published in 1858: "Anti-Proudhonist Ideas about Love, Woman and Marriage"; and later, in Germany, a book titled *The Antifeminists* (1902) by Hedwig Dohm (1831–1919).

"Our enemies come at us from above as from below. By which I mean: they can justify their opposition by reference to either the spiritual or bodily inferiority of Woman, or else, disguise it by invoking the lofty mission of Woman as the mother-priestess of home and hearth, her tender gentleness and all the rest of it. The majority, however, deploy both tactics simultaneously: belt and braces, as it were. For the most part—leaving aside, of course, all ethical and aesthetic feelings of repugnance—their argumentation consists of mere assertion."—Hedwig Dohm

At the US women's conference in 1851, the itinerant preacher and former slave Sojourner Truth (1798–1883) gave one of the most impressive speeches of the time, which not only debunked the idea of "positive discrimination" favoring women as a "weaker" sex in need of protection, but simultaneously denounced the racism inherent in those bourgeois clichés about gender in the first place.

Three topical concerns preoccupied the emerging women's unions and women's groups of that era: the demand for better access to paid work; the critique of traditional households and the injustice of forced marriage (a critique often bound up with ideas of "free love"); and the demand for universal suffrage.

WOMEN'S WAGE LABOR

The most important issue for women's movements in the 19th century was women's entry into the wage labor market. In fact, at the outset of industrialization—which began in the textiles sector—the majority of workers had been women.

But the more factory work grew in general importance, the more the male workers' associations and labor unions demanded a ban or at least restrictions on female factory work. The First International (1864–1872) itself—the first umbrella organization representing the European laboring class—passed motions along these lines at its first congresses, and only arrived at a more moderate position later on.

Meanwhile, among bourgeois women, the situation looked different . . .

For this reason, the question of access to adequately paid and respectable opportunities for wage labor occupied a central position in almost all feminist activities during these years. Feminists organized practical initiatives for self-help, discussed the issue in economic terms, and set up lobbies to push for the appropriate political measures.

In doing so, they mostly rejected all so-called "women's protection laws" that legally prohibited women from working certain jobs on account of their (supposedly fragile) physical constitutions or their capacity to give birth. Here's one example out of many:

We, a few activists from England, have founded the Society for Promoting the Employment of Women. That was last year, in 1859 . . .

and this year it's borne fruit in the form of this printing press in London: the Victoria Press.

As you can see, the Press is made up entirely of women!

Here, the workers can even train to become printers themselves.

Because the pay in our branch is relatively good.

The initiative encountered massive opposition from male printers and trade unions, especially since the venture played hardball when it came to setting prices to attract clients.

In Germany, one journalist and feminist who advocated passionately for women's right to wage labor was Louise Otto-Peters (1819–1895). She launched the *Women's Newspaper* in 1849 (under the famous motto "I am recruiting female citizens for the realm of freedom!"), but went on to found workers' and servants' unions too, and published her book *Women's Right to Earn a Living* in 1866.

Together with others, Otto-Peters organized the first German women's conference in Leipzig in 1865. She directed the General German Women's Union for three decades after that—which offered, for instance, advanced training courses for women.

My objective is, on the one hand, to support women workers in realizing their right to paid work, and, at the same time, to win them over as comrades in the struggle for women's political rights.

"Gentlemen! In the name of morality, in the name of the fatherland, in the name of humanity I appeal to you: when it comes to the organization of labor, do not forget women!"—Louise Otto-Peters

Finally, some important theorists of women's paid labor were Harriet Taylor Mill (1807–1858) and her daughter Helen Taylor (1831–1907).

Together with the theorist of liberal political economy John Stuart Mill, which is to say, their husband and stepfather (respectively), they authored numerous texts on economics, as well as on suffrage rights and divorce rights. Their approach to capitalism was utilitarian and oriented toward the "greatest good of the greatest number."

For indeed, women's free participation in labor markets will increase the wealth of any nation!

The close link between the liberal conception of the economy and the demand for unrestricted equality for women is present in all of the Mills's works, but is most explicitly formulated in 1869 in the collectively authored book *The Subjection of Women* (which, however, appeared solely under John Stuart's name).

Are you sure we should do this without your names?

Yes. If we publish under your name, our ideas will gain more recognition and provoke more attention.

"The legal subordination of one sex to the other is wrong in itself, and now one of the chief hindrances to human improvement."—John Stuart Mill, Harriet Taylor Mill, and Helen Taylor

FREE LOVE / THE CRITIQUE OF MARRIAGE

Another crucial theme in the 19th century was the plight of wives. In most European countries, marriage meant a mass transfer of entitlements from bride to groom, and married women lost practically all their rights.

> Will you honor and obey this man, in sickness and in health, until death do you part?

> Yes, she will!

> And cede unto him your choice of living place, control over your your assets, and possibly also your income, in the event that he gives your permission to work? If so, answer now: "I will."

> HUHH??

"Husband and wife are one and that is he." (From England's law ordinance on marriage.)

> At the time, when it came to marriage, what kind of choice did a bourgeois woman really have?

> Marriage for me was the only possible source of food. Now, without my husband's written permission, I cannot sign any contracts, do any kind of business, appear as a witness in court, nor even travel abroad. And of course he has full, unilateral decision-making power over everything to do with our children.

It was particularly extreme in France, where the Code Civil even expressly prohibited husbands from granting general power of attorney to their wives. Sharing power of attorney had been a key strategy for enlightened couples, not least for practical reasons. Getting a divorce was basically impossible in France, and subject to strict conditions in other countries as well—all of which worked to the disadvantage of the woman. The situation was slightly different in Germany. Until 1874, German weddings were almost exclusively administered by the churches (who often denied people the right to marry).

These marriage laws affected women of different social classes in different ways.

We proletarian women often live with men, outside of marriage, and it is not uncommon for us to then choose other men, or women, to be our life partners.

In our households there simply isn't anything worth inheriting or distributing, so what would be the point of a big song and dance around marriage?

Sex before marriage, for example, just isn't a big deal as far as we're concerned. It's pregnancy you have to worry about. After all, pregnancy has financial implications.

Besides, it was much rarer for people from the proletarian class to hash out their differences before the courts, and deviations from the classical institution of marriage were simply not regarded as particularly scandalous.

In contrast, the bourgeoisie placed enormous emphasis on womanly "respectability." When bourgeois women left their husbands, they faced not only poverty but the loss of their children and the severance of all their social connections. For this reason, the reform of marriage law was really only a concern for bourgeois feminists—the more so because it also encompassed their right to inherit.

If I get a divorce, I will lose the assets I inherited from my father. I am not legally competent to own them in the eyes of the law.

While their attempts at reform remained unsuccessful in France throughout the 19th century, in England the issue was vigorously debated and campaigners secured a couple of ameliorations in 1857 and 1870.

Many feminists did not care particularly about the legal ins and outs of marriage, but wanted to mount a critique of the sexual morality underlying the laws. Some, like the French writer George Sand (1804–1876), led promiscuous lifestyles and did not hide this from the public. Others, such as the US feminist and socialist Victoria Woodhull (1838–1927), went on the offensive and demanded women's right to sexual autonomy.

"Yes, I am a Free Lover. I have an inalienable, constitutional and natural right to love whom I may, to love as long or as short a period as I can; to change that love every day if I please, and with that right neither you nor any law you can frame have any right to interfere."
—Victoria Woodhull

The Russian "Nihilists," many of whose members used to travel to Western Europe at the time to study, elicited a particularly strong public reaction. They organized a lot of fake weddings between themselves and like-minded men, because single women were not permitted to leave Russia. They advocated dissolving all gendered norms, refused to wear typically feminine clothing, and cultivated a "masculine" lifestyle and habitus.

Within feminism itself, such practices were not met with undivided support. Only a minority of advocates for women's rights wanted to abolish the traditional family entirely. With regard to "free love," the various women's associations and unions did not pull together by any means; they even fought each other over it.

In Germany, for example, by the end of the 19th century three distinct streams had emerged:

The "Radicals" around Minna Cauer (1841–1922), Lida Gustava Heymann (1868–1943), Anita Augspurg (1857–1943), and Helene Stöcker (1869–1943) ...

We demand a new sexual moral order, and a social status for women that is entirely unrelated to marriage.

... the "Moderates" around Helene Lange (1848–1930) and Gertrud Bäumer (1873–1954) ...

We are certainly also for the abolition of forced marriages and unjust laws. Nevertheless, we hold woman's social role as a mother to be important. The aims of feminist emancipation must have their limits.

... and, finally, the "Conservatives," who wanted to valorize the "housewife's vocation" and had no fundamental criticisms of the marital system.

WOMEN'S RIGHT TO VOTE AND PARTY POLITICS

The feminist positions around voting rights were just as polarized. This campaign, too, lay closest to bourgeois women's hearts. In the 19th century, in many countries, the right to vote was still tied to property or land assets, so that most proletarian men were equally as shut out from voting as were women of all classes.

Moreover, many socialist currents, for instance anarchism, aimed at more radical forms of social revolution and generally opposed circumscribing workers' struggles within party apparatuses and the horizons of parliamentary politics.

In the United States, this question even led to a split in the women's movement. There, after the end of the Civil War between the Northern and Southern states in 1869, suffrage rights were introduced for black men—but not for women.

Your privileges? Soon enough you will try to offer us those dull trinkets, in an attempt to restore their former luster by sharing them with us. Keep them, we don't want them.

Which is not to say that we will tolerate that happening in the South! We would rather support votes for women!

Louise Michel, French anarchist (1830–1905)

Many feminists still welcomed this change, because they considered it an important step for the black population. On the other hand, radical women's rights advocates like Susan B. Anthony (1820–1906) or Elizabeth Cady Stanton (1815–1902) were indignant, because they now foresaw women's suffrage being kicked even further down the road as a result. Nor did they shy away from the crudest forms of racism in making their complaint, for instance when they ridiculed the fact that "Sambo" was now allowed to vote, while educated ladies could not. Elizabeth Cady Stanton opined . . .

Toward the end of the 19th century, feminists supported the fight for women's suffrage in ever greater numbers, and increasingly found that they had allies among men. Those most often making the headlines were the English suffragettes, whose imaginative direct action and downright militancy forced the issue into the mainstream. The time had well and truly come: in almost all nation-states, women were admitted into the electorate, for example in 1902 in Australia, 1906 in Finland, 1913 in Norway, 1915 in Denmark, 1918 in Poland, Germany, and Austria, 1920 in the United States, 1928 in the UK, 1930 in Turkey, 1945 in France and Italy, and 1971 in Switzerland.

One of the lasting consequences of debates around women's suffrage was a stronger focus on women's relationship to political party structures.

Now that you're a voter, and you can run for political office, who will enjoy your loyalty? Your party, to whom you feel you belong politically ... ?

... or perhaps we should put our hopes in a cross-party women's federation.

The beginning of the 20th century saw the proliferation of women's associations specifically affiliated with particular political parties or religious denominations. For example, one of the greatest contributors to socialist feminist organizing in Germany at the time was Clara Zetkin (1857–1933) and her newspaper *Equality*.

The bourgeois women's movement is not the representative or champion of the interests of all women who long for liberation. It is and remains a bourgeois class movement.

These women advocated within their organizations for the rights and interests of women, while simultaneously attempting to win other women over to their worldview. Even if they did sometimes forge alliances with one another's organizations, they refused—again and again—to see one another as a vehicle of women's true interests.

Others, like the Russian-American activist Emma Goldman (1869–1940) had no time at all for institutional organizing, but she was, after all, an anarchist in the first instance and a feminist only second. Or was it the other way around?

You've seen what the women's movement for voting rights looks like. A bourgeois movement that is, in large part, conservative, puritanical, and even racist. You're asking me not to be suspicious of such a movement?

And if voting changed anything, it would be banned!

I want to see women as free human beings, people who are free in equal measure from the state, the church, society, husbands, family, etc.

Naturally some women are hoping to free themselves from all of that with the help of the right to vote. But who really profits from all this, more than anyone? The majority of women are hoping that the vote helps them become better Christians, housewives, and bourgeois citizens.

In any case, the tension between political orientation, on the one hand, and the desire for solidarity among women across or beyond ideological lines, on the other, has been a constant (and thorny) issue in feminism ever since.

THE "OTHER" SEX?

A further problem that cropped up in tandem with the introduction of women's suffrage was the realization that formal rights did not necessarily ameliorate the social situation for women. The French philosopher Simone de Beauvoir (1908–1986) wrote the major groundbreaking book on this theme in 1949.

Even nowadays it's still alleged that there is some kind of natural essence of woman.

I have never felt myself to be inferior. So far I have always lived my life unconventionally and independently. Nevertheless, "being a woman" relegates every woman to secondary status.

In *The Second Sex*, she examines Western European cultural and philosophical history in order to show that gender roles are hammered out, not only on the level of legislation, but in literature, morality, and everyday custom.

"For a long time I have hesitated to write a book on woman. The subject is irritating, especially to women; and it is not new. After all, is there a problem? And if so, what is it? Are there women, really?"—Simone de Beauvoir

"*One is not born but rather becomes a woman*" is probably de Beauvoir's most famous line. According to this perspective, the concept of sex is shaped by culture, and does not simply inhere in "*the nature of things.*"

Nor did she conceal the reality that women's passive and subordinate role is not solely assigned to them by men; in fact, women play a major part in maintaining it.

Half victim, half accomplice, just like everybody else.

Politically, she demanded that women be liberated from their social role as mothers, above all; she called on women to put more energy into their professional or political careers and to take steps to ensure that gender differences would disappear from society by and by.

But Simone de Beauvoir became a major icon of feminism only around twenty years later, when she was rediscovered by a newly reinvigorated women's movement.

Now, as then, a majority of feminists share de Beauvoir's cultural analysis. But not everybody agrees with the conclusions she drew. One of those to take issue with them was the French psychoanalyst Luce Irigaray (1930–).

De Beauvoir holds up the male mode of living as though it were the norm, and simply calls on women to adapt themselves to it.

In her 1974 book *Speculum of the Other Woman*, Irigaray demonstrates that masculinity does not merely structure culture: rather, it undergirds the very "symbolic order" and language itself.

Women must now find a language of their own and build a free feminine subjectivity. Only then will it be possible for men and women to enter into a relationship with one another.

In order for the fact of sexual difference to be realized, there will have to be a revolution in thought and ethics. Everything must be signified anew, but we must begin with the Subject, who has hitherto always been specified as masculine, even if we have pretended that it was neutral and universal.

These two positions gave rise to a broad and ever-evolving feminist debate about the relation between "equality" and "difference"—a debate that is still going on today.

The greatest evil is actually the presumption of a "difference between the sexes" in the first place!

I agree. I'm for gender equality! I reject all these notions of motherly love.

How nice for you! Go ahead! With that attitude all you're doing is assimilating to the masculine subject, instead of developing a genuine femininity of your own.

Exactly. Our emphasis on "more femininity" can be a useful tool for promoting subversion of the hegemonic masculinist norms. Let's look for inspiration to the world's matriarchal cultures!...

One often encounters truncated, simplistic
representations of the conflict between "equality feminism"
and "difference feminism." It is certainly true that "equality feminists"
have sometimes submitted themselves rather uncritically to the norm of the
masculine, and that, on the other hand, some "difference feminists" have posited such a thing
as women's "natural" being. Nevertheless, both sides have contributed considerable wisdom to the
navigation of this unresolved territory between the poles of "equality" and "difference."

AUTONOMOUS WOMEN'S MOVEMENTS

In tandem with the student movements of the end of the 1960s in the United States and Europe, an autonomous women's movement reconstituted itself as well. "Autonomous" here refers to the fact that the feminists no longer felt committed to their organizations, parties, or religious denominations, but turned instead toward a form of consciousness based on self-organizing simply as women. This turn was prompted by their frustrations about even the most "revolutionary" mixed movements being dominated by men.

In Germany, the filmmaker Helke Sander (1937–) helped found the Action Committee for the Liberation of Women.

If you SDS members are serious, and we proceed on that assumption, then it is only logical that our groups should work together, and that you support us.

Oh, whatever. This is actually a classic example of an ancillary contradiction.

Feminism is so petty-bourgeois.

Yup! It only weakens and divides anticapitalist struggle.

In Frankfurt in September 1968, at a plenary meeting of the radical leftist group SDS, this conflict infamously broke out in the form of a "tomato attack." After Sander had given a speech putting forward the demands of the Action Committee, the men summarily tried to switch over to other topics without any further discussion. So, Sigrid Rüger, who was in the audience, threw a tomato that happened to be in her shopping bag at the comrades on the speaker's platform, forcing even the most reluctant to have the discussion.

"After we'd been active for about half a year, most comrades still reacted to what we were doing with scorn. Today, they resent the fact that we withdrew from their movements. They still want to tell us that our social theorizing is completely wrongheaded to begin with. They bang on about how they are oppressed too, which of course isn't news to us. We just aren't willing to put up with their oppression's priority anymore. Their oppression is itself the means by which they oppress us—and we have suffered it without a murmur."

—Helke Sander

Umm . . . yes, how many tomatoes will you be needing this time?

A WHOLE LOT !

In the 1970s, the praxis of "separatism" led to a groundswell of women's groups, women's bookstores, and women's cafés, not only in metropolitan areas, but also in many small towns. It was US feminists who invented "consciousness-raising," whereby women would speak among themselves, sharing their experiences with each other and reflecting on them politically. Women's groups in many other countries also adopted this practice.

Lesbian women played a vital role in the "second wave" of feminism. Many of the women who pioneered the new projects were lesbians, perhaps because, since they were already conducting their private relationships in a "woman-identified" way, their everyday lives could easily be combined with feminist-separatist praxis. Of course, women had lived together as couples long before that (for example, Lida Gustava Heymann and Anita Augspurg), but during the first wave no one had turned their lesbianism into a subject for political discussion.

The theorization of lesbianism was hugely advanced by the French writer Monique Wittig (1935–2005). From her point of view, lesbians were not women at all: *"it would be incorrect to say that lesbians associate, make love, live with women, for 'woman' has meaning only in heterosexual systems of thought and heterosexual economic systems. Lesbians are not women."*

In the course of their feminist engagements, lesbians also intensified their criticisms of men's dominance within the gay movement.

For us, it's not about getting acceptance for "same-sex love."

We want sexed concepts to be challenged in general!

Many of us think of our lesbianism not so much as a sexual identity, but as a political statement.

OK. Are you ready now?

Uh-huh. I think so.

Women, who had previously lived their love for other women in secret, now made their relationships public.

Others who had previously lived with men and also poured their energies into motherhood now decided—as a result of their engagement with the feminist movement—to share their intimate lives with women as well. Such people were known as "movement lesbians." As one popular slogan put it:

At the beginning of the 1980s, the US poet and cultural theorist Adrienne Rich (1929–2012) developed the concept of the "lesbian continuum." She directed her analysis at "compulsory heterosexuality" and posited that female homosexuality is taboo—in a patriarchal culture—because it reveals the belief that women can only find true fulfillment in a relationship with a man to be a lie. As such, according to Rich, lesbianism really concerns all women.

"I mean the term lesbian continuum to include a range—through each woman's life and throughout history—of woman-identified experience; not simply the fact that a woman has had or consciously desired genital sexual experience with another woman."
—Adrienne Rich

Soon thereafter, feminist magazines proliferated, the most well-known ones in Germany being *Courage* (1976–1984) and *Emma* (founded 1977), which is still publishing today.

This intense period of awakening for feminists in the 1970s is often called "the second wave" (after the first wave, the fight for women's voting rights).

In terms of political content, three main battlegrounds became particularly important during this time. All are mutually interrelated: claiming bodily self-determination as a fundamental right; revolutionizing parenting, housework, and domestic labor; and blowing the lid off the scandal of epidemic sexual violence in society.

THE FIGHT FOR AUTONOMOUS PREGNANCY

In April 1971, nearly 350 French women—including celebrities such as Catherine Deneuve and Jeanne Moreau—publicly disclosed the fact that they had had abortions in the pages of *Le Nouvel Observateur*. In Germany, Alice Schwarzer (1942–) initiated an identical intervention in *Stern* magazine in June 1971, in which Senta Berger and Romy Schneider, among others, struck a blow against the nationwide ban on abortion.

Not all of the women who started speaking up about abortion, unashamed, had had abortions themselves. The campaign was really much more a question of demonstrating that the power to make choices about pregnancy concerns all women.

In the United States, feminists supported a class action against the abortion ban in the state of Texas. The Supreme Court had ruled in the case of *Roe v. Wade* in 1973 that any law prohibiting women from having an abortion is unconstitutional as long as the fetus is unable to live on its own.

In East Germany in 1972, the People's Parliament legalized abortion during the first three months of pregnancy. Then, in West Germany, the Parliament resolved in 1974 to follow suit and implement this type of first-trimester legalization. However, that law was buried soon after by the German Constitutional Court.

In some countries today, a "de facto" first-trimester limit on abortion persists. This means that abortion, while officially illegal, is not subject to prosecution under penal law as long as pregnant women conform to certain limits and are willing, for example, to accept counseling.

Abortion after twelve weeks is only legitimate and legal when strictly medical, eugenic, or criminological criteria determine the pregnancy to be "unacceptable for the woman."

That makes it sound like getting an abortion in that time frame is simple and straightforward for everybody. In reality, you have to pay for the procedure yourself, except in so-called "special cases."

I recently heard about a young woman in the United States who tried to crowd-fund her abortion online.

I'm not surprised. I'm denied medical care entirely just because my legal status in this country is irregular. Pregnancy, birth, and—for that matter—abortion would all be very difficult for me.

Some feminists considered the focus on pregnancy a narrowing of contemporary debates. They felt other topics warranted more attention within the feminist struggle. Some of them specifically resented that the demands connected with pregnancy didn't go far enough. The US activist Shulamith Firestone (1945–2012) had already argued for the total abolition of the biological family in her 1970 book *The Dialectic of Sex*, which soon became a best-seller.

In Firestone's vision, people would live in communities in which no special attachment exists between a given mother and child. One of her utopian demands was the transcendence of biological pregnancy by means of reproductive technology. In this way, a society would emerge in which gender differences would no longer play any role.

"Feminists have to question, not just all of Western culture, but the organization of culture itself, and further, even the very organization of nature."
— Shulamith Firestone

Aside from pursuing political demands, women in the 1970s also elaborated systems of practical support. They organized trips to places like the Netherlands, where abortion was legal. They educated themselves and each other about methods of contraception, founded women's health centers, and explored their own bodies—for example, by examining their own vaginas.

DOMESTIC VIOLENCE

A feminist group in the 1970s . . .

I'd never have thought that so many members of our group were experiencing violence in their marriage or domestic partnership.

The second big task in the so-called second wave of feminist activism was to expose domestic violence against women and children.

People are only now beginning to realize that homes are actively dangerous places for many women, and in no sense sanctuaries, as we commonly imagined.

MY HOME IS MY CASTLE

Instances of rape and battery that take place within a marriage are widely understood to be private matters, not criminal acts.

My best bet is to stay silent. If I don't he'll get angry!

And many of the women victimized thought their case was the exception.

She probably provoked him!

You know what marriage is like. Now and then there's fireworks—it's only natural.

The testimonies shared in women's centers and consciousness-raising groups planted the seeds of widespread sensitization to the fact that violence within families isn't limited to individual incidents, but represents a structural problem.

Accordingly, in almost every city in that period, feminists set up independent women's crisis services and shelters, where victims of domestic violence could take refuge without having to file bureaucratic appeals.

On a political level, activists put their energy into criminalizing rape within marriage.

In 1997, German criminal law was finally amended, making rape within marriage a crime. In the intervening time, many of the autonomous women's refuges and advice centers feminists had set up in the 1970s for victims of violence passed into municipal hands or started receiving public funding.

HOUSEWORK, CARE, MOTHERHOOD

The third central theme of second-wave feminism was the critique of the gendered division of labor. Broadly speaking, within homes, men were in charge of earning money, and women were in charge of (unpaid) housework and the (unpaid) work of raising children.

The Action Committee for the Liberation of Women had called for the abolition of the bourgeois compartmentalization of private life and social life. Its founder Helke Sander was also the cofounder of the "Kinderladen" (playschool) movement, in which mothers and preschool educators conceived of alternative institutions for collectivizing childcare and launched initiatives along those lines. The point of all this was not simply to render the organization of care labor and housework independent of the state. The movement was experimenting with new concepts in liberatory pedagogy—rooted in antiauthoritarian principles—which took the children seriously as subjects.

There was considerable disagreement about the way housework and child care should ideally be structured and economically organized. Some demanded "Wages for Housework," not simply to guarantee housewives an income of their own, but to expose housework's centrality to the national economy. (These feminists' contention, that the ensemble of unpaid cooking, cleaning, washing, and parenting that took place within households constituted real "work" was a radical new idea at the time.) Others demanded that housework and paid work be distributed equally between the sexes; or that housework be thoroughgoingly centralized and professionalized. Over the course of these debates, the putative "naturalness" of motherhood as women's vocation in life and the idea of their innate capacity for care were fatally undermined.

In 1987, a group of women affiliated with the Green Party in Germany published a "Mother's Manifesto," in which they advocated basic economic security for unpaid mothers and the social valorization of housework. Their critics accused them of reinforcing gender stereotypes.

Women! Abandon the ghetto of childlessness and break free of the aquarium of "career womanhood"!

Motherhood isn't just a burden, it's also joy and fulfillment!

In order to make women work for nothing, one cannot very well extol the beauty and glamor of washing dishes and doing the laundry by way of enticement. So, instead, you tell them about the joy of motherhood.

Simone de Beauvoir (1908–1986)

In actual fact, society developed in the direction of "gender mainstreaming," the province of paid labor, while housework and care continues to be regarded to this day as a private matter. This priority of paid over unpaid work was entrenched via corresponding changes in the law—for example, substantial reductions in the right to alimony, and the neoliberal reform of children's benefits.

Women's increasing involvement in paid work in the 1990s and 2000s certainly delivered more economic independence and security for some women. But the problem remains that the parameters within which housekeeping and child care take place are highly precarious; in fact, this precarity has only grown worse. While women today work exponentially more paid hours than they did in the 1960s and '70s, men hardly spend more time now than they used to on housekeeping and child care.

So, the question is: who shall do the job formerly known as "housewife," when there are no more housewives? This is a question we still haven't answered. The current situation generates huge amounts of stress because of the "double burden" or "double shift" for mothers who have careers. Other consequences include the outsourcing of all kinds of domestic services to migrant women, who toil under precarious and often legally ambiguous conditions in private households; and—on the other hand—the delegation of care to public institutions, where the high costs incurred often translate into low wages and terrible contracts for the people working in that sector, not to mention poor-quality service.

In all this time, feminist initiatives have continued to grapple with the issue of care. In March 2014, a high-profile political event in Berlin titled "Care Revolution" brought together all the strands of this discussion. A network emerged, which continues to make every effort to put care at the heart of political conversations.

WOMANISM AND INTERSECTIONALITY
AGAINST THE DOMINANCE OF WHITE, BOURGEOIS WOMEN

* A 1932 law in the United States provided a mandate for forced sterilization. In practice, the policy became a vector for the racist population politics espoused by the government. Those affected were overwhelmingly indigenous, Chicana, Puerto Rican, and African-American women.

As early as the 1960s, more and more women raised their voices in criticism of the dominance of a white, bourgeois perspective on women's rights, for example the poet Audre Lorde (1934–1992)...

"If white American feminist theory need not deal with the differences between us, and the resulting difference in our oppressions, then how do you deal with the fact that the women who clean your houses and tend your children while you attend conferences on feminist theory are, for the most part, poor women and women of color?"

... or the philosopher Angela Davis (1944–), whose book *Women, Race, and Class* was published in 1981.

"As a black woman, my politics and political affiliation are bound up with and flow from participation in my people's struggle for liberation, and with the fight of oppressed people all over the world."

66

To underline these differences, black activist women coined the term "womanism." The linked nature of different relations of discrimination was also dealt with at the time under the term "triple oppression" (which meant the threefold oppression on the basis of sex, skin color, and class affiliation).

At the end of the 1980s, the legal theorist Kimberlé Crenshaw (1959–) coined the term "intersectionality," that is, crossroads. It speaks to the fact that different forms of discrimination can't just be added up: a person is discriminated against as a woman, a person of color, and a lesbian—a lesbian woman of color—all at once. The different axes of oppression are so interlinked that the specific character of each individual aspect transforms the others as well. For example, a black woman is treated differently as a woman than a white woman is.

The terminology proliferates . . .

CLASS ETHNICITY GENDER SEXUAL ORIENTATION BODY NORMS

INTERSECTIONALITY

RACE AGE ETC.

Originally, there were the three categories of race, class, and gender.

We cannot simply lift the American category of race and apply it to the European context.

Furthermore, it soon became clear that besides these three, numerous other kinds of systemic injustice demanded analysis, for example, discrimination on the basis of sexual orientation, bodily norms, age, and so on.

Today, in feminism, taking an intersectional approach is basically indispensable. At the same time, things are not going so smoothly. .

GENDER MAINSTREAMING AND THE PROMOTION OF WOMEN

In the 1980s, women in many countries began to advocate for the de facto equality for women within political institutions, and to launch corresponding legal initiatives.

The United Nations' Fourth World Conference on Women in Beijing in 1995 went down in history as a red-letter day. Official delegates from 189 countries took part. The result of the discussions was a platform through which the nation-states committed themselves to promoting equality between women and men in the political, economic, and social spheres; fighting against women's poverty; and condemning all forms of violence against women. The distinction between sex and gender proved key to this political project—that is to say, the distinction between biological characteristics and social assignment (or presentation). The UN emphasized that social norms and patterns of behavior cannot be extrapolated from biological male- or femaleness and that these norms, in fact, evolve via socialization and upbringing.

Since then, legislators have written many equivalent laws, on a national and Europe-wide level. Through "Gender Mainstreaming," the European Union requires its member states to "mainstream" their practice in keeping with a specific perspective on sex-participation. This means they have to constantly consider whether policies might affect women and men differently. Many institutions started hiring permanent women's advocates and equal opportunities officers.

In the beginning, these jobs had been occupied by women with roots in the autonomous women's movements. Their ambition was to carry separatist-feminist politics into societies' institutions. But over time, it came to be bureaucrats and civil servants who took up these posts—women, and sometimes men, who didn't even necessarily see themselves as feminists.

LIBERATION, NOT EQUALIZATION

However, among feminists, there was a divided reaction to the institutionalization of feminist demands. Many rejected the idea that women could liberate themselves by means of "equalization" and adaptation to a male-dominated culture and its rules. Critics raised objections to the idea that a subject position based on unconditional solidarity between women—"We the Women"—even existed, from which one could level demands.

Among the first to contradict the universalizing claims of mainstream feminism was Audre Lorde, in a speech given to white academic women in 1984. Lorde demanded that her audience take the differences between women seriously, suggesting that difference, in itself, should become the starting point for feminist activism.

> *Our respective (nondominant) differences are interdependent.*

> *"Within that mutual interdependence lies that security which enables us to find true visions of our future. Difference is that raw and powerful connection from which our personal power is forged."*—Audre Lorde

In Europe, the pioneers of this nonessentialist "difference feminism" are the Italian feminists of the Women's Bookstore in Milan, and the "Diotima" community of women-philosophers in Verona. In 1989, in the book *How Feminist Freedom Arises*, the Milanese authorial collective postulates that the freedom of women stems from meaningful and strong relationships with other women. One of the most important exponents of this tendency is the philosopher Luisa Muraro (1940–).

"From the relationships among women and the liberation of our desire, we have learned of the existence of many strengths and potentialities that only need to be unleashed: powers that can help us to make the condition of womanhood freer, better and more pleasant. But then, the political parties, the Left, the state, and the European Union introduced this idea of 'equality' into feminism. Instead of women creating a new society, they made us believe that we have to take power."
—Luisa Muraro

Instead of investing themselves in a politics of demands (vis-à-vis the state, political establishment, and men), the Italian feminists proposed that women should share authority over their dreams and their projects exclusively with other women. This idea, known as "Affidamento" (confidence or entrustment), has become famous in Germany too.

QUEER FEMINISM

Simultaneously, many feminists began to fundamentally question the categories of "male" and "female" as well.

Oh, she's getting soaked!

Well, too bad. She's not a real woman.

No she isn't! You can't just buy your way into woman's identity with a few hormone tablets, after all.

Fine. Then I guess I'll just get an umbrella of my own.

. . . Then again, many did not.

The struggle in the 1960s that took place at the Stonewall Inn on Christopher Street in New York is widely acknowledged to be a seminal moment for queer politics. It was here that those excluded from the haunts of well-to-do gays and lesbians congregated: trans people, drag queens, LGBTI people of color, sex-workers, and homeless people.

It was they who were hit hardest by the violent raids that happened daily in the so-called "gay bars." Today, all around the world, events are held on "Christopher Street Day" to commemorate their resistance to this racist, transphobic, classist, and homophobic police violence.

In 1990 the influential book *Gender Trouble* was released, in which the philosopher Judith Butler (1956–) coined the term "heterosexual Matrix."

The term describes the assumption that there are precisely two unequivocally definable sexes, whose desires are mutually complementary.

People who did not want to conform to this binary sex logic adopted the term "queer"—which roughly means "strange, crazy, outside of every norm"—to describe themselves in a positive sense.

"'Biological sex' is an ideological construct that is coercively materialized over time. It is not a plain fact of the body, nor a static situation, but rather a process, by which regulatory norms materialize this 'biological sex,' and achieve this materialization by means of enforced and incessant repetition of these norms."
—Judith Butler

While, at first, it was above all lesbians and gays who called themselves "queer"—because they lived and loved outside the heterosexual norm—the word later became a collective term for the general diversity of sexual identities.

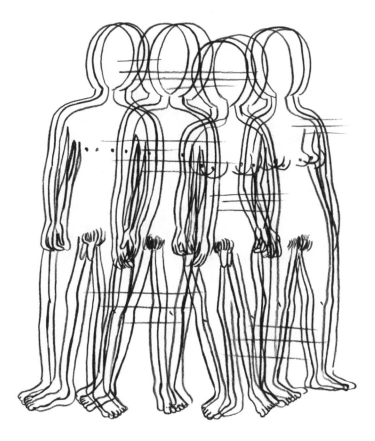

Today, the term "queer" encompasses inter-sexuality (which designates people who lack an unambiguous sex designation), transsexuality (people whose gender is different from the one that was assigned to them at birth), bisexuality (people who desire both men and women), and so on. To refer to all of these identities together there are acronyms such as LGBTQI (Lesbian Gay Bisexual Trans Queer Intersex)—a list that is by no means exhaustive, since new additions can always be made.

Originally wary of excluding people through its very acts of inclusion, the politics of "queer" has now become, more often than not, a label of identity.

THIRD-WAVE FEMINISM

So, since the women's movement in the 1980s was splitting off in various directions, it began to lose some of its cohesive power. At the same time, new countermovements appeared against feminism's achievements. Some men began countercampaigns aimed at safeguarding their privileges. The journalist Susan Faludi (1959–) analyzed this trend in her book *Backlash* in 1991. Meanwhile, some women considered feminism to be outdated because equal rights had been achieved; they called themselves "postfeminists."

Next, in opposition to these prevailing trends, a new movement began to form in the United States. It is sometimes called the "third wave."

The term comes from America. It goes back to a plea expressed by Rebecca Walker, the daughter (born in 1969) of the famous novelist Alice Walker.
In reaction to a court sentence acquitting a rapist, she wrote in 1992:

"I write this as a plea to all women, especially the women of my generation: Let this dismissal of a woman's experience move you to anger. Turn that outrage into political power. Do not vote for them unless they work for us. Do not have sex with them, do not break bread with them, do not nurture them if they don't prioritize our freedom to control our bodies and our lives. I am not a postfeminism feminist. I am the Third Wave."

Out of this movement, various projects developed that combined (for example) pop culture and feminism, like the "riot grrrls" and publications like *Missy Magazine* in Germany, which was launched in 2008.

The division of feminism into separate "waves" is problematic in many respects. Within any of the groups designated as a "wave," people have promoted very different ideologies. Even so, there are several ways in which the themes of the third wave tend to distinguish themselves from the second. Third wavers reject the idea of a fundamental antagonism between women and men. They criticize any suggestion of "natural" femininity ...

... and are skeptical of traditional forms of politics, favoring looser forms of organization and networking—for instance, via the internet.